The Pilgrims Of Hope And Chants For Socialists

William Morris

THE PILGRIMS OF HOPE

AND

CHANTS FOR SOCIALISTS

BY

WILLIAM MORRIS

LONGMANS, GREEN & COMPANY
39 PATERNOSTER ROW, LONDON
FOURTH AVENUE & 30TH STREET, NEW YORK
BOMBAY, CALCUTTA, AND MADRAS
1915

FOREWORD

"The Pilgrims of Hope" appeared in *The Commonweal* between March 1885 and July 1886, its title being decided on with the publication of the second part. Sections I, IV, and VIII were included in *Poems by the Way* after the author had abandoned his intention of revising it as a whole. "To be concluded" stands at the bottom of the last instalment.

"Chants for Socialists," consisting of songs and poems written for various occasions and collected into a penny pamphlet published by the Socialist League in 1885, is here printed entire (with the exception of "The Message of the March Wind," pp. 3–6), although "The Day is Coming," "The Voice of Toil," and "All for the Cause," were included in *Poems by the Way*. "A Death Song," which also appears there, was written for the funeral of Alfred Linnell, who died from injuries received at a Demonstration in Trafalgar Square on November 20, 1887. It first appeared in pamphlet form, with a musical setting by Malcolm Lawson.

"May Day" [1892] and "May Day, 1894," appeared in *Justice*.

CONTENTS

THE PILGRIMS OF HOPE:

		PAGE
THE MESSAGE OF THE MARCH WIND	. . . . .	3
THE BRIDGE AND THE STREET	. . . . .	7
SENDING TO THE WAR	. . . . . .	11
MOTHER AND SON	. . . . . .	15
NEW BIRTH	. . . .	19
THE NEW PROLETARIAN	. . . . . .	24
IN PRISON—AND AT HOME	. . . . .	30
THE HALF OF LIFE GONE	. . . . .	35
A NEW FRIEND	. . . . . .	39
READY TO DEPART	. . . . .	43
A GLIMPSE OF THE COMING DAY	. . . .	47
MEETING THE WAR-MACHINE	. . . . .	51
THE STORY'S ENDING	. . . . . .	54

CHANTS FOR SOCIALISTS:

THE DAY IS COMING	. . . .	61
THE VOICE OF TOIL	. . . . . .	65
NO MASTER	. . . .	67

CHANTS FOR SOCIALISTS (*continued*)—

PAGE

    ALL FOR THE CAUSE 68

    THE MARCH OF THE WORKERS 70

    DOWN AMONG THE DEAD MEN 73

A DEATH SONG 75

MAY DAY [1892] 77

MAY DAY, 1894 80

THE PILGRIMS OF HOPE

I

THE MESSAGE OF THE MARCH WIND

FAIR now is the springtide, now earth lies beholding
 With the eyes of a lover the face of the sun;
Long lasteth the daylight, and hope is enfolding
 The green-growing acres with increase begun.

Now sweet, sweet it is through the land to be straying
 Mid the birds and the blossoms and the beasts of the field;
Love mingles with love, and no evil is weighing
 On thy heart or mine, where all sorrow is healed.

From township to township, o'er down and by tillage
 Far, far have we wandered and long was the day,
But now cometh eve at the end of the village,
 Where over the grey wall the church riseth grey.

There is wind in the twilight; in the white road before us
 The straw from the ox-yard is blowing about;
The moon's rim is rising, a star glitters o'er us,
 And the vane on the spire-top is swinging in doubt.

Down there dips the highway, toward the bridge crossing over
 The brook that runs on to the Thames and the sea.
Draw closer, my sweet, we are lover and lover;
 This eve art thou given to gladness and me.

Shall we be glad always? Come closer and hearken:
   Three fields further on, as they told me down there,
When the young moon has set, if the March sky should darken,
   We might see from the hill-top the great city's glare.

Hark, the wind in the elm-boughs! From London it bloweth,
   And telling of gold, and of hope and unrest;
Of power that helps not; of wisdom that knoweth,
   But teacheth not aught of the worst and the best.

Of the rich men it telleth, and strange is the story
   How they have, and they hanker, and grip far and wide;
And they live and they die, and the earth and its glory
   Has been but a burden they scarce might abide.

Hark! the March wind again of a people is telling;
   Of the life that they live there, so haggard and grim,
That if we and our love amidst them had been dwelling
   My fondness had faltered, thy beauty grown dim.

This land we have loved in our love and our leisure
   For them hangs in heaven, high out of their reach;
The wide hills o'er the sea-plain for them have no pleasure,
   The grey homes of their fathers no story to teach.

The singers have sung and the builders have builded,
   The painters have fashioned their tales of delight;
For what and for whom hath the world's book been gilded,
   When all is for these but the blackness of night?

How long and for what is their patience abiding?
  How oft and how oft shall their story be told,
While the hope that none seeketh in darkness is hiding
  And in grief and in sorrow the world groweth old?

COME back to the inn, love, and the lights and the fire,
  And the fiddler's old tune and the shuffling of feet;
For there in a while shall be rest and desire,
  And there shall the morrow's uprising be sweet.

Yet, love, as we wend the wind bloweth behind us
  And beareth the last tale it telleth to-night,
How here in the spring-tide the message shall find us;
  For the hope that none seeketh is coming to light.

Like the seed of midwinter, unheeded, unperished,
  Like the autumn-sown wheat 'neath the snow lying green,
Like the love that o'ertook us, unawares and uncherished,
  Like the babe 'neath thy girdle that groweth unseen,

So the hope of the people now buddeth and groweth—
  Rest fadeth before it, and blindness and fear;
It biddeth us learn all the wisdom it knoweth;
  It hath found us and held us, and biddeth us hear:

For it beareth the message: "Rise up on the morrow
  And go on your ways toward the doubt and the strife;
Join hope to our hope and blend sorrow with sorrow,
  And seek for men's love in the short days of life."

But lo, the old inn, and the lights and the fire,
    And the fiddler's old tune and the shuffling of feet;
Soon for us shall be quiet and rest and desire,
    And to-morrow's uprising to deeds shall be sweet.

II

THE BRIDGE AND THE STREET

In the midst of the bridge there we stopped and we wondered
   In London at last, and the moon going down,
All sullied and red where the mast-wood was sundered
   By the void of the night-mist, the breath of the town.

On each side lay the City, and Thames ran between it
   Dark, struggling, unheard 'neath the wheels and the feet.
A strange dream it was that we ever had seen it,
   And strange was the hope we had wandered to meet.

Was all nought but confusion? What man and what master
   Had each of these people that hastened along?
Like a flood flowed the faces, and faster and faster
   Went the drift of the feet of the hurrying throng.

Till all these seemed but one thing, and we twain another,
   A thing frail and feeble and young and unknown;
What sign mid all these to tell foeman from brother?
   What sign of the hope in our hearts that had grown?

We went to our lodging afar from the river,
   And slept and forgot—and remembered in dreams;
And friends that I knew not I strove to deliver
   From a crowd that swept o'er us in measureless streams,

7

Wending whither I knew not: till meseemed I was waking
  To the first night in London, and lay by my love,
And she worn and changed, and my very heart aching
  With a terror of soul that forbade me to move.

Till I woke, in good sooth, and she lay there beside me,
  Fresh, lovely in sleep; but awhile yet I lay,
For the fear of the dream-tide yet seemed to abide me
  In the cold and sad time ere the dawn of the day.

Then I went to the window, and saw down below me
  The market-wains wending adown the dim street,
And the scent of the hay and the herbs seemed to know me,
  And seek out my heart the dawn's sorrow to meet.

They passed, and day grew, and with pitiless faces
  The dull houses stared on the prey they had trapped;
'Twas as though they had slain all the fair morning places
  Where in love and in leisure our joyance had happed.

My heart sank; I murmured, "What's this we are doing
  In this grim net of London, this prison built stark
With the greed of the ages, our young lives pursuing
  A phantom that leads but to death in the dark?"

Day grew, and no longer was dusk with it striving,
  And now here and there a few people went by.
As an image of what was once eager and living
  Seemed the hope that had led us to live or to die.

Yet nought else seemed happy; the past and its pleasure
  Was light, and unworthy, had been and was gone;
If hope had deceived us, if hid were its treasure,
  Nought now would be left us of all life had won.

O LOVE, stand beside me; the sun is uprisen
  On the first day of London; and shame hath been here.
For I saw our new life like the bars of a prison,
  And hope grew a-cold, and I parleyed with fear.

Ah! I sadden thy face, and thy grey eyes are chiding!
  Yea, but life is no longer as stories of yore;
From us from henceforth no fair words shall be hiding
  The nights of the wretched, the days of the poor.

Time was we have grieved, we have feared, we have faltered,
  For ourselves, for each other, while yet we were twain;
And no whit of the world by our sorrow was altered,
  Our faintness grieved nothing, our fear was in vain.

Now our fear and our faintness, our sorrow, our passion,
  We shall feel all henceforth as we felt it erewhile;
But now from all this the due deeds we shall fashion
  Of the eyes without blindness, the heart without guile.

Let us grieve then—and help every soul in our sorrow;
  Let us fear—and press forward where few dare to go;
Let us falter in hope—and plan deeds for the morrow,
  The world crowned with freedom, the fall of the foe.

As the soldier who goes from his homestead a-weeping,
    And whose mouth yet remembers his sweetheart's embrace,
While all round about him the bullets are sweeping,
    But stern and stout-hearted dies there in his place;

Yea, so let our lives be! e'en such that hereafter,
    When the battle is won and the story is told,
Our pain shall be hid, and remembered our laughter,
    And our names shall be those of the bright and the bold.

NOTE.—This section had the following note in *The Commonweal:* It is the intention of the author to follow the fortunes of the lovers who in the "Message of the March Wind" were already touched by sympathy with the cause of the people.

III

SENDING TO THE WAR

It was down in our far-off village that we heard of the war begun,
But none of the neighbours were in it save the squire's thick-lipped son,
A youth and a fool and a captain, who came and went away,
And left me glad of his going. There was little for us to say
Of the war and its why and wherefore—and we said it often enough;
The papers gave us our wisdom, and we used it up in the rough.
But I held my peace and wondered; for I thought of the folly of men,
The fair lives ruined and broken that ne'er could be mended again;
And the tale by lies bewildered, and no cause for a man to choose;
Nothing to curse or to bless—just a game to win or to lose.

But here were the streets of London—strife stalking wide in the world;
And the flag of an ancient people to the battle-breeze unfurled.
And who was helping or heeding? The gaudy shops displayed
The toys of rich men's folly, by blinded labour made;
And still from naught to nothing the bright-skinned horses drew
Dull men and sleek-faced women with never a deed to do;
While all about and around them the street-flood ebbed and flowed,
Worn feet, grey anxious faces, grey backs bowed 'neath the load.
Lo the sons of an ancient people! And for this they fought and fell
In the days by fame made glorious, in the tale that singers tell.

We two we stood in the street in the midst of a mighty crowd,
The sound of its mingled murmur in the heavens above was loud,
And earth was foul with its squalor—that stream of every day,
The hurrying feet of labour, the faces worn and grey,
Were a sore and grievous sight, and enough and to spare had I seen
Of hard and pinching want midst our quiet fields and green;
But all was nothing to this, the London holiday throng.
Dull and with hang-dog gait they stood or shuffled along,
While the stench from the lairs they had lain in last night went up in
     the wind,
And poisoned the sun-lit spring: no story men can find
Is fit for the tale of their lives; no word that man hath made
Can tell the hue of their faces, or their rags by filth o'er-laid:
For this hath our age invented—these are the sons of the free,
Who shall bear our name triumphant o'er every land and sea.
Read ye their souls in their faces, and what shall help you there?
Joyless, hopeless, shameless, angerless, set is their stare:
This is the thing we have made, and what shall help us now,
For the field hath been laboured and tilled and the teeth of the dragon
     shall grow.

But why are they gathered together? what is this crowd in the street?
This is a holiday morning, though here and there we meet
The hurrying tradesman's broadcloth, or the workman's basket of tools.
Men say that at last we are rending the snares of knaves and fools ;
That a cry from the heart of the nation against the foe is hurled,
And the flag of an ancient people to the battle-breeze unfurled.
The soldiers are off to the war, we are here to see the sight,
And all our griefs shall be hidden by the thought of our country's might.
'Tis the ordered anger of England and her hope for the good of the Earth
That we to-day are speeding, and many a gift of worth

Shall follow the brand and the bullet, and our wrath shall be no curse,
But a blessing of life to the helpless—unless we are liars and worse—
And these that we see are the senders; these are they that speed
The dread and the blessing of England to help the world at its need.

Sick unto death was my hope, and I turned and looked on my dear,
And beheld her frightened wonder, and her grief without a tear,
And knew how her thought was mine—when, hark! o'er the hubbub
    and noise,
Faint and a long way off, the music's measured voice,
And the crowd was swaying and swaying, and somehow, I knew not why,
A dream came into my heart of deliverance drawing anigh.
Then with roll and thunder of drums grew the music louder and loud,
And the whole street tumbled and surged, and cleft was the holiday crowd,
Till two walls of faces and rags lined either side of the way.
Then clamour of shouts rose upward, as bright and glittering gay
Came the voiceful brass of the band, and my heart beat fast and fast,
For the river of steel came on, and the wrath of England passed
Through the want and the woe of the town, and strange and wild was
    my thought,
And my clenched hands wandered about as though a weapon they sought.

Hubbub and din was behind them, and the shuffling haggard throng,
Wandering aimless about, tangled the street for long;
But the shouts and the rhythmic noise we still heard far away,
And my dream was become a picture of the deeds of another day.
Far and far was I borne, away o'er the years to come,
And again was the ordered march, and the thunder of the drum,
And the bickering points of steel, and the horses shifting about
'Neath the flashing swords of the captains—then the silence after the
    shout—

Sun and wind in the street, familiar things made clear,
Made strange by the breathless waiting for the deeds that are drawing
    anear.
For woe had grown into will, and wrath was bared of its sheath,
And stark in the streets of London stood the crop of the dragon's teeth.
Where then in my dream were the poor and the wall of faces wan?
Here and here by my side, shoulder to shoulder of man,
Hope in the simple folk, hope in the hearts of the wise,
For the happy life to follow, or death and the ending of lies,
Hope is awake in the faces angerless now no more,
Till the new peace dawn on the world, the fruit of the people's war.

War in the world abroad a thousand leagues away,
While custom's wheel goes round and day devoureth day.
Peace at home!—what peace, while the rich man's mill is strife,
And the poor is the grist that he grindeth, and life devoureth life?

IV

MOTHER AND SON

Now sleeps the land of houses, and dead night holds the street,
And there thou liest, my baby, and sleepest soft and sweet;
My man is away for awhile, but safe and alone we lie;
And none heareth thy breath but thy mother, and the moon looking
    down from the sky
On the weary waste of the town, as it looked on the grass-edged road
Still warm with yesterday's sun, when I left my old abode,
Hand in hand with my love, that night of all nights in the year;
When the river of love o'erflowed and drowned all doubt and fear,
And we two were alone in the world, and once, if never again,
We knew of the secret of earth and the tale of its labour and pain.

Lo amidst London I lift thee, and how little and light thou art,
And thou without hope or fear, thou fear and hope of my heart!
Lo here thy body beginning, O son, and thy soul and thy life;
But how will it be if thou livest, and enterest into the strife,
And in love we dwell together when the man is grown in thee,
When thy sweet speech I shall hearken, and yet 'twixt thee and me
Shall rise that wall of distance, that round each one doth grow,
And maketh it hard and bitter each other's thought to know?
Now, therefore, while yet thou art little and hast no thought of thine own,
I will tell thee a word of the world, of the hope whence thou hast grown,

15

Of the love that once begat thee, of the sorrow that hath made
Thy little heart of hunger, and thy hands on my bosom laid.
Then mayst thou remember hereafter, as whiles when people say
All this hath happened before in the life of another day;
So mayst thou dimly remember this tale of thy mother's voice,
As oft in the calm of dawning I have heard the birds rejoice,
As oft I have heard the storm-wind go moaning through the wood,
And I knew that earth was speaking, and the mother's voice was good.

Now, to thee alone will I tell it that thy mother's body is fair,
In the guise of the country maidens who play with the sun and the air,
Who have stood in the row of the reapers in the August afternoon,
Who have sat by the frozen water in the highday of the moon,
When the lights of the Christmas feasting were dead in the house on the
   hill,
And the wild geese gone to the salt marsh had left the winter still.
Yea, I am fair, my firstling; if thou couldst but remember me!
The hair that thy small hand clutcheth is a goodly sight to see;
I am true, but my face is a snare; soft and deep are my eyes,
And they seem for men's beguiling fulfilled with the dreams of the wise.
Kind are my lips, and they look as though my soul had learned
Deep things I have never heard of. My face and my hands are burned
By the lovely sun of the acres; three months of London-town
And thy birth-bed have bleached them indeed—"But lo, where the edge
   of the gown"
(So said thy father one day) "parteth the wrist white as curd
From the brown of the hands that I love, bright as the wing of a bird."

Such is thy mother, O firstling, yet strong as the maidens of old,
Whose spears and whose swords were the warders of homestead, of field
   and of fold.

Oft were my feet on the highway, often they wearied the grass;
From dusk unto dusk of the summer three times in a week would I pass
To the downs from the house on the river through the waves of the blos-
   soming corn.
Fair then I lay down in the even, and fresh I arose on the morn,
And scarce in the noon was I weary. Ah, son, in the days of thy strife,
If thy soul could harbour a dream of the blossom of my life!
It would be as sunlit meadows beheld from a tossing sea,
And thy soul should look on a vision of the peace that is to be.

Yet, yet the tears on my cheek! And what is this doth move
My heart to thy heart, beloved, save the flood of yearning love?
For fair and fierce is thy father, and soft and strange are his eyes
That look on the days that shall be with the hope of the brave and the
   wise.
It was many a day that we laughed as over the meadows we walked,
And many a day I hearkened and the pictures came as he talked;
It was many a day that we longed, and we lingered late at eve
Ere speech from speech was sundered, and my hand his hand could leave.
Then I wept when I was alone, and I longed till the daylight came;
And down the stairs I stole, and there was our housekeeping dame
(No mother of me, the foundling) kindling the fire betimes
Ere the haymaking folk went forth to the meadows down by the limes ;
All things I saw at a glance; the quickening fire-tongues leapt
Through the crackling heap of sticks, and the sweet smoke up from it crept,
And close to the very hearth the low sun flooded the floor,
And the cat and her kittens played in the sun by the open door.
The garden was fair in the morning, and there in the road he stood
Beyond the crimson daisies and the bush of southernwood.
Then side by side together through the grey-walled place we went,
And O the fear departed, and the rest and sweet content!

B

Son, sorrow and wisdom he taught me, and sore I grieved and learned
As we twain grew into one; and the heart within me burned
With the very hopes of his heart. Ah, son, it is piteous,
But never again in my life shall I dare to speak to thee thus;
So may these lonely words about thee creep and cling,
These words of the lonely night in the days of our wayfaring.
Many a child of woman to-night is born in the town,
The desert of folly and wrong; and of what and whence are they grown?
Many and many an one of wont and use is born;
For a husband is taken to bed as a hat or a ribbon is worn.
Prudence begets her thousands: "Good is a housekeeper's life,
So shall I sell my body that I may be matron and wife."
"And I shall endure foul wedlock and bear the children of need."
Some are there born of hate—many the children of greed.
" I, I too can be wedded, though thou my love hast got."
" I am fair and hard of heart, and riches shall be my lot."
And all these are the good and the happy, on whom the world dawns fair.
O son, when wilt thou learn of those that are born of despair,
As the fabled mud of the Nile that quickens under the sun
With a growth of creeping things, half dead when just begun?
E'en such is the care of Nature that man should never die,
Though she breed of the fools of the earth, and the dregs of the city sty.
But thou, O son, O son, of very love wert born,
When our hope fulfilled bred hope, and fear was a folly outworn ;
On the eve of the toil and the battle all sorrow and grief we weighed,
We hoped and we were not ashamed, we knew and we were not afraid.

Now waneth the night and the moon—ah, son, it is piteous
That never again in my life shall I dare to speak to thee thus.
But sure from the wise and the simple shall the mighty come to birth;
And fair were my fate, beloved, if I be yet on the earth
When the world is awaken at last, and from mouth to mouth they tell
Of thy love and thy deeds and thy valour, and thy hope that nought can quel

V

NEW BIRTH

It was twenty-five years ago that I lay in my mother's lap
New born to life, nor knowing one whit of all that should hap:
That day was I won from nothing to the world of struggle and pain,
Twenty-five years ago—and to-night am I born again.

I look and behold the days of the years that are passed away,
And my soul is full of their wealth, for oft were they blithe and gay
As the hours of bird and of beast: they have made me calm and strong
To wade the stream of confusion, the river of grief and wrong.

A rich man was my father, but he skulked ere I was born,
And gave my mother money, but left her life to scorn;
And we dwelt alone in our village: I knew not my mother's "shame,"
But her love and her wisdom I knew till death and the parting came.
Then a lawyer paid me money, and I lived awhile at a school,
And learned the lore of the ancients, and how the knave and the fool
Have been mostly the masters of earth: yet the earth seemed fair and good
With the wealth of field and homestead, and garden and river and wood;
And I was glad amidst it, and little of evil I knew
As I did in sport and pastime such deeds as a youth might do,
Who deems he shall live for ever. Till at last it befel on a day
That I came across our Frenchman at the edge of the new-mown hay,
A-fishing as he was wont, alone as he always was;

So I helped the dark old man to bring a chub to grass,
And somehow he knew of my birth, and somehow we came to be friends,
Till he got to telling me chapters of the tale that never ends;
The battle of grief and hope with riches and folly and wrong.
He told how the weak conspire, he told of the fear of the strong;
He told of dreams grown deeds, deeds done ere time was ripe,
Of hope that melted in air like the smoke of his evening pipe;
Of the fight long after hope in the teeth of all despair;
Of battle and prison and death, of life stripped naked and bare.
But to me it all seemed happy, for I gilded all with the gold
Of youth that believes not in death, nor knoweth of hope grown cold.
I hearkened and learned, and longed with a longing that had no name,
Till I went my ways to our village and again departure came.

Wide now the world was grown, and I saw things clear and grim,
That awhile agone smiled on me from the dream-mist doubtful and dim.
I knew that the poor were poor, and had no heart or hope;
And I knew that I was nothing with the least of evils to cope;
So I thought the thoughts of a man, and I fell into bitter mood,
Wherein, except as a picture, there was nought on the earth that was good;
Till I met the woman I love, and she asked, as folk ask of the wise,
Of the root and meaning of things that she saw in the world of lies.
I told her all I knew, and the tale told lifted the load
That made me less than a man; and she set my feet on the road.

So we left our pleasure behind to seek for hope and for life,
And to London we came, if perchance there smouldered the embers of
 strife
Such as our Frenchman had told of; and I wrote to him to ask
If he would be our master, and set the learners their task.
But "dead" was the word on the letter when it came back to me,
And all that we saw henceforward with our own eyes must we see.

So we looked and wondered and sickened; not for ourselves indeed:
My father by now had died, but he left enough for my need;
And besides, away in our village the joiner's craft had I learned,
And I worked as other men work, and money and wisdom I earned.
Yet little from day to day in street or workshop I met
To nourish the plant of hope that deep in my heart had been set.
The life of the poor we learned, and to me there was nothing new
In their day of little deeds that ever deathward drew.
But new was the horror of London that went on all the while
That rich men played at their ease for name and fame to beguile
The days of their empty lives, and praised the deeds they did,
As though they had fashioned the earth and found out the sun long hid;
Though some of them busied themselves from hopeless day to day
With the lives of the slaves of the rich and the hell wherein they lay.
They wrought meseems as those who should make a bargain with hell,
That it grow a little cooler, and thus for ever to dwell.

So passed the world on its ways, and weary with waiting we were.
Men ate and drank and married; no wild cry smote the air,
No great crowd ran together to greet the day of doom;
And ever more and more seemed the town like a monstrous tomb
To us, the Pilgrims of Hope, until to-night it came,
And Hope on the stones of the street is written in letters of flame.

This is how it befel: a workmate of mine had heard
Some bitter speech in my mouth, and he took me up at the word,
And said: "Come over to-morrow to our Radical spouting-place;
For there, if we hear nothing new, at least we shall see a new face;
He is one of those Communist chaps, and 'tis like that you two may agree."
So we went, and the street was as dull and as common as aught you could see;
Dull and dirty the room. Just over the chairman's chair
Was a bust, a Quaker's face with nose cocked up in the air;

There were common prints on the wall of the heads of the party fray,
And Mazzini dark and lean amidst them gone astray.
Some thirty men we were of the kind that I knew full well,
Listless, rubbed down to the type of our easy-going hell.
My heart sank down as I entered, and wearily there I sat
While the chairman strove to end his maunder of this and of that.
And partly shy he seemed, and partly indeed ashamed
Of the grizzled man beside him as his name to us he named.
He rose, thickset and short, and dressed in shabby blue,
And even as he began it seemed as though I knew
The thing he was going to say, though I never heard it before.
He spoke, were it well, were it ill, as though a message he bore,
A word that he could not refrain from many a million of men.
Nor aught seemed the sordid room and the few that were listening then
Save the hall of the labouring earth and the world which was to be.
Bitter to many the message, but sweet indeed unto me,
Of man without a master, and earth without a strife,
And every soul rejoicing in the sweet and bitter of life:
Of peace and good-will he told, and I knew that in faith he spake,
But his words were my very thoughts, and I saw the battle awake,
And I followed from end to end; and triumph grew in my heart
As he called on each that heard him to arise and play his part
In the tale of the new-told gospel, lest as slaves they should live and die.

He ceased, and I thought the hearers would rise up with one cry,
And bid him straight enrol them; but they, they applauded indeed,
For the man was grown full eager, and had made them hearken and heed:
But they sat and made no sign, and two of the glibber kind
Stood up to jeer and to carp his fiery words to blind.
I did not listen to them, but failed not his voice to hear
When he rose to answer the carpers, striving to make more clear
That which was clear already; not overwell, I knew,

He answered the sneers and the silence, so hot and eager he grew;
But my hope full well he answered, and when he called again
On men to band together lest they live and die in vain,
In fear lest he should escape me, I rose ere the meeting was done,
And gave him my name and my faith—and I was the only one.
He smiled as he heard the jeers, and there was a shake of the hand,
He spoke like a friend long known; and lo! I was one of the band.

And now the streets seem gay and the high stars glittering bright;
And for me, I sing amongst them, for my heart is full and light.
I see the deeds to be done and the day to come on the earth,
And riches vanished away and sorrow turned to mirth;
I see the city squalor and the country stupor gone.
And we a part of it all—we twain no longer alone
In the days to come of the pleasure, in the days that are of the fight—
I was born once long ago: I am born again to-night.

VI

THE NEW PROLETARIAN

How near to the goal are we now, and what shall we live to behold?
Will it come a day of surprise to the best of the hopeful and bold?
Shall the sun arise some morning and see men falling to work,
Smiling and loving their lives, not fearing the ill that may lurk
In every house on their road, in the very ground that they tread?
Shall the sun see famine slain, and the fear of children dead?
Shall he look adown on men set free from the burden of care,
And the earth grown like to himself, so comely, clean and fair?
Or else will it linger and loiter, till hope deferred hath spoiled
All bloom of the life of man—yea, the day for which we have toiled?
Till our hearts be turned to stone by the griefs that we have borne,
And our loving kindness seared by love from our anguish torn.
Till our hope grow a wrathful fire, and the light of the second birth
Be a flame to burn up the weeds from the lean impoverished earth.

What's this? Meseems it was but a little while ago
When the merest sparkle of hope set all my heart aglow!
The hope of the day was enough; but now 'tis the very day
That wearies my hope with longing. What's changed or gone away?
Or what is it drags at my heart-strings?—is it aught save the coward's
    fear?
In this little room where I sit is all that I hold most dear—

My love, and the love we have fashioned, my wife and the little lad.
Yet the four walls look upon us with other eyes than they had,
For indeed a thing hath happened. Last week at my craft I worked,
Lest oft in the grey of the morning my heart should tell me I shirked;
But to-day I work for us three, lest he and she and I
In the mud of the street should draggle till we come to the workhouse
    or die.

Not long to tell is the story, for, as I told you before,
A lawyer paid me the money which came from my father's store.
Well, now the lawyer is dead, and a curious tangle of theft,
It seems, is what he has lived by, and none of my money is left.
So I who have worked for my pleasure now work for utter need:
In "the noble army of labour" I now am a soldier indeed.

"You are young, you belong to the class that you love," saith the rich
    man's sneer;
"Work on with your class and be thankful." All that I hearken to hear,
Nor heed the laughter much; have patience a little while,
I will tell you what's in my heart, nor hide a jot by guile.
When I worked pretty much for my pleasure I really worked with a will,
It was well and workmanlike done, and my fellows knew my skill,
And deemed me one of themselves though they called me gentleman Dick,
Since they knew I had some money; but now that to work I must stick,
Or fall into utter ruin, there's something gone, I find;
The work goes, cleared is the job, but there's something left behind;
I take up fear with my chisel, fear lies 'twixt me and my plane,
And I wake in the merry morning to a new unwonted pain.
That's fear: I shall live it down—and many a thing besides
Till I win the poor dulled heart which the workman's jacket hides.
Were it not for the Hope of Hopes I know my journey's end,
And would wish I had ne'er been born the weary way to wend.

Now,further, well you may think we have lived no gentleman's life,
My wife is my servant, and I am the servant of my wife,
And we make no work for each other; but country folk we were,
And she sickened sore for the grass and the breath of the fragrant air
That had made her lovely and strong; and so up here we came
To the northern slopes of the town to live with a country dame,
Who can talk of the field-folks' ways: not one of the newest the house,
The woodwork worn to the bone, its panels the land of the mouse,
Its windows rattling and loose, its floors all up and down;
But this at least it was, just a cottage left in the town.
There might you sit in our parlour in the Sunday afternoon
And watch the sun through the vine-leaves and fall to dreaming that
    soon
You would see the grey team passing, their fetlocks wet with the brook,
Or the shining mountainous straw-load: there the summer moon would
    look
Through the leaves on the lampless room, wherein we sat we twain,
All London vanished away; and the morn of the summer rain
Would waft us the scent of the hay; or the first faint yellow leaves
Would flutter adown before us and tell of the acres of sheaves.

All this hath our lawyer eaten, and to-morrow must we go
To a room near my master's shop, in the purlieus of Soho.
No words of its shabby meanness! But that is our prison-cell
In the jail of weary London. Therein for us must dwell
The hope of the world that shall be, that rose a glimmering spark
As the last thin flame of our pleasure sank quavering in the dark.

Again the rich man jeereth: "The man is a coward, or worse—
He bewails his feeble pleasure; he quails before the curse
Which many a man endureth with calm and smiling face."
Nay, the man is a man, by your leave! Or put yourself in his place,

And see if the tale reads better. The haven of rest destroyed,
And nothing left of the life that was once so well enjoyed
But leave to live and labour, and the glimmer of hope deferred.
Now know I the cry of the poor no more as a story heard,
But rather a wordless wail forced forth from the weary heart.
Now, now when hope ariseth I shall surely know my part.

THERE's a little more to tell. When those last words were said,
At least I was yet a-working, and earning daily bread.
But now all that is changed, and meseems adown the stair
That leads to the nethermost pit, man, wife and child must fare.

When I joined the Communist folk, I did what in me lay
To learn the grounds of their faith. I read day after day
Whatever books I could handle, and heard about and about
What talk was going amongst them; and I burned up doubt after doubt,
Until it befel at last that to others I needs must speak
(Indeed, they pressed me to that while yet I was weaker than weak).
So I began the business, and in street-corners I spake
To knots of men. Indeed, that made my very heart ache,
So hopeless it seemed; for some stood by like men of wood;
And some, though fain to listen, but a few words understood;
And some but hooted and jeered: but whiles across some I came
Who were keen and eager to hear; as in dry flax the flame
So the quick thought flickered amongst them: and that indeed was a feast.
So about the streets I went, and the work on my hands increased;
And to say the very truth betwixt the smooth and the rough
It was work and hope went with it, and I liked it well enough:
Nor made I any secret of all that I was at
But daily talked in our shop and spoke of this and of that.

Then vanished my money away, and like a fool I told
Some one or two of the loss. Did that make the master bold?
Before I was one of his lot, and as queer as my head might be
I might do pretty much as I liked. Well now he sent for me
And spoke out in very words my thought of the rich man's jeer:
"Well, sir, you have got your wish, as far as I can hear,
And are now no thief of labour, but an honest working man:
Now I'll give you a word of warning: stay in it as long as you can,
This working lot that you like so: you're pretty well off as you are.
So take another warning: I have thought you went too far,
And now I am quite sure of it; so make an end of your talk
At once and for ever henceforth, or out of my shop you walk;
There are plenty of men to be had who are quite as good as you.
And mind you, anywhere else you'll scarce get work to do,
Unless you rule your tongue;—good morning; stick to your work."

The hot blood rose to my eyes, somewhere a thought did lurk
To finish both him and the job: but I knew now what I was,
And out of the little office in helpless rage did I pass
And went to my work, a *slave*, for the sake of my child and my sweet.
Did men look for the brand on my forehead that eve as I went through
    the street?
And what was the end after all? Why, one of my shopmates heard
My next night's speech in the street, and passed on some bitter word,
And that week came a word with my money: "You needn't come again."
And the shame of my four days' silence had been but grief in vain.

Well I see the days before me: this time we shall not die
Nor go to the workhouse at once: I shall get work by-and-by,
And shall work in fear at first, and at last forget my fear,
And drudge on from day to day, since it seems that I hold life dear.

'Tis the lot of many millions! Yet if half of those millions knew
The hope that my heart hath learned, we should find a deed to do,
And who or what should withstand us? And I, e'en I might live
To know the love of my fellows and the gifts that earth can give.

VII

IN PRISON—AND AT HOME

THE first of the nights is this, and I cannot go to bed;
I long for the dawning sorely, although when the night shall be dead,
Scarce to me shall the day be alive. Twice twenty-eight nights more,
Twice twenty-eight long days till the evil dream be o'er!
And he, does he count the hours as he lies in his prison-cell?
Does he nurse and cherish his pain? Nay, I know his strong heart well,
Swift shall his soul fare forth; he is here, and bears me away,
Till hand in hand we depart toward the hope of the earlier day.
Yea, here or there he sees it: in the street, in the cell, he sees
The vision he made me behold mid the stems of the blossoming trees,
When spring lay light on the earth, and first and at last I knew
How sweet was his clinging hand, how fair were the deeds he would do.

Nay, how wilt thou weep and be soft and cherish a pleasure in pain,
When the days and their task are before thee and awhile thou must work
    for twain?
O face, thou shalt lose yet more of thy fairness, be thinner no doubt,
And be waxen white and worn by the day that he cometh out!
Hand, how pale thou shalt be! how changed from the sunburnt hand
That he kissed as it handled the rake in the noon of the summer land!

Let me think then it is but a trifle: the neighbours have told me so;
"Two months! why that is nothing and the time will speedily go."

'Tis nothing—O empty bed, let me work then for his sake!
I will copy out the paper which he thought the News might take,
If my eyes may see the letters; 'tis a picture of our life
And the little deeds of our days ere we thought of prison and strife.

Yes, neighbour, yes I am early—and I was late last night;
Bedless I wore through the hours and made a shift to write.
It was kind of you to come, nor will it grieve me at all
To tell you why he's in prison and how the thing did befal;
For I know you are with us at heart, and belike will join us soon.
It was thus: we went to a meeting on Saturday afternoon,
At a new place down in the West, a wretched quarter enough,
Where the rich men's houses are elbowed by ragged streets and rough,
Which are worse than they seem to be. (Poor thing! you know too well
How pass the days and the nights within that bricken hell!)
There, then, on a bit of waste we stood 'twixt the rich and the poor;
And Jack was the first to speak; that was he that you met at the door
Last week. It was quiet at first; and dull they most of them stood
As though they heeded nothing, nor thought of bad or of good,
Not even that they were poor, and haggard and dirty and dull:
Nay, some were so rich indeed that they with liquor were full,
And dull wrath rose in their souls as the hot words went by their ears,
For they deemed they were mocked and rated by men that were more
    than their peers.
But for some, they seemed to think that a prelude was all this
To the preachment of saving of souls, and hell, and endless bliss;
While some (O the hearts of slaves!) although they might understand,
When they heard their masters and feeders called thieves of wealth and
    of land,
Were as angry as though *they* were cursed. Withal there were some that
    heard,
And stood and pondered it all, and garnered a hope and a word.

Ah! heavy my heart was grown as I gazed on the terrible throng.
Lo! these that should have been the glad and the deft and the strong,
How were they dull and abased as the very filth of the road!
And who should waken their souls or clear their hearts of the load?

The crowd was growing and growing, and therewith the jeering grew;
And now that the time was come for an ugly brawl I knew,
When I saw how midst of the workmen some well-dressed men there
    came,
Of the scum of the well-to-do, brutes void of pity or shame;
The thief is a saint beside them, These raised a jeering noise,
And our speaker quailed before it, and the hubbub drowned his voice.
Then Richard put him aside and rose at once in his place,
And over the rags and the squalor beamed out his beautiful face,
And his sweet voice rang through the tumult, and I think the crowd
    would have hushed
And hearkened his manly words; but a well-dressed reptile pushed
Right into the ring about us and screeched out infamies
That sickened the soul to hearken; till he caught my angry eyes
And my voice that cried out at him, and straight on me he turned,
A foul word smote my heart and his cane on my shoulders burned.
But e'en as a kestrel stoops down Richard leapt from his stool
And drave his strong right hand amidst the mouth of the fool.
Then all was mingled together, and away from him was I torn,
And, hustled hither and thither, on the surging crowd was borne;
But at last I felt my feet, for the crowd began to thin,
And I looked about for Richard that away from thence we might win;
When lo, the police amidst us, and Richard hustled along
Betwixt a pair of blue-coats as the doer of all the wrong!

Little longer, friend, is the story; I scarce have seen him again;
I could not get him bail despite my trouble and pain;

And this morning he stood in the dock: for all that that might avail,
They might just as well have dragged him at once to the destined jail.
The police had got their man and they meant to keep him there,
And whatever tale was needful they had no trouble to swear.

Well, the white-haired fool on the bench was busy it seems that day,
And so with the words "Two months," he swept the case away;
Yet he lectured my man ere he went, but not for the riot indeed
For which he was sent to prison, but for holding a dangerous creed.
"What have you got to do to preach such perilous stuff?
To take some care of yourself should find you work enough.
If you needs must preach or lecture, then hire a chapel or hall;
Though indeed if you take my advice you'll just preach nothing at all,
But stick to your work: you seem cleyer; who knows but you might rise,
And become a little builder should you condescend to be wise?
For in spite of your silly sedition, the land that we live in is free,
And opens a pathway to merit for you as well as for me."

Ah, friend, am I grown light-headed with the lonely grief of the night,
That I babble of this babble? Woe's me, how little and light
Is this beginning of trouble to all that yet shall be borne—
At worst but as the shower that lays but a yard of the corn
Before the hailstorm cometh and flattens the field to the earth.

O for a word from my love of the hope of the second birth!
Could he clear my vision to see the sword creeping out of the sheath
Inch by inch as we writhe in the toils of our living death!
Could he but strengthen my heart to know that we cannot fail;
For alas, I am lonely here—helpless and feeble and frail;
I am e'en as the poor of the earth, e'en they that are now alive;
And where is their might and their cunning with the mighty of men to
    strive?

C

Though they that come after be strong to win the day and the crown,
Ah, ever must we the deedless to the deedless dark go down,
Still crying, "To-morrow, to-morrow, to-morrow yet shall be
The new-born sun's arising o'er happy earth and sea"—
And we not there to greet it—for to-day and its life we yearn,
And where is the end of toiling and whitherward now shall we turn
But to patience, ever patience, and yet and yet to bear;
And yet, forlorn, unanswered as oft before to hear,
Through the tales of the ancient fathers and the dreams that mock our
     wrong,
That cry to the naked heavens, "How long, O Lord! how long?"

VIII

THE HALF OF LIFE GONE

THE days have slain the days, and the seasons have gone by
And brought me the summer again; and here on the grass I lie
As erst I lay and was glad ere I meddled with right and with wrong.
Wide lies the mead as of old, and the river is creeping along
By the side of the elm-clad bank that turns its weedy stream,
And grey o'er its hither lip the quivering rushes gleam.
There is work in the mead as of old; they are eager at winning the hay,
While every sun sets bright and begets a fairer day.
The forks shine white in the sun round the yellow red-wheeled wain,
Where the mountain of hay grows fast; and now from out of the lane
Comes the ox-team drawing another, comes the bailiff and the beer,
And thump, thump, goes the farmer's nag o'er the narrow bridge of the weir.
High up and light are the clouds, and though the swallows flit ·
So high o'er the sunlit earth, they are well a part of it,
And so, though high over them, are the wings of the wandering herne;
In measureless depths above him doth the fair sky quiver and burn;
The dear sun floods the land as the morning falls toward noon,
And a little wind is awake in the best of the latter June.

They are busy winning the hay, and the life and the picture they make,
If I were as once I was, I should deem it made for my sake;
For here if one need not work is a place for happy rest,
While one's thought wends over the world, north, south, and east and west.

There are the men and the maids, and the wives and the gaffers grey
Of the fields I know so well, and but little changed are they
Since I was a lad amongst them; and yet how great is the change!
Strange are they grown unto me; yea, I to myself am strange.
Their talk and their laughter mingling with the music of the meads
Has now no meaning to me to help or to hinder my needs,
So far from them have I drifted. And yet amidst them goes
A part of myself, my boy, and of pleasure and pain he knows,
And deems it something strange when he is other than glad.
Lo now! the woman that stoops and kisses the face of the lad,
And puts a rake in his hand and laughs in his laughing face—
Whose is the voice that laughs in the old familiar place?
Whose should it be but my love's, if my love were yet on the earth?
Could she refrain from the fields where my joy and her joy had birth,
When I was there and her child, on the grass that knew her feet
Mid the flowers that led her on when the summer eve was sweet?

No, no, it is she no longer; never again can she come
And behold the hay-wains creeping o'er the meadows of her home;
No more can she kiss her son or put the rake in his hand
That she handled a while agone in the midst of the haymaking band.
Her laughter is gone and her life; there is no such thing on the earth,
No share for me then in the stir, no share in the hurry and mirth.

Nay, let me look and believe that all these will vanish away,
At least when the night has fallen, and that she will be there mid the hay,
Happy and weary with work, waiting and longing for love.
There will she be, as of old, when the great moon hung above,
And lightless and dead was the village, and nought but the weir was awake;
There will she rise to meet me, and my hands will she hasten to take,
And thence shall we wander away, and over the ancient bridge
By many a rose-hung hedgerow, till we reach the sun-burnt ridge

And the great trench digged by the Romans: there then awhile shall we
  stand,
To watch the dawn come creeping o'er the fragrant lovely land,
Till all the world awaketh, and draws us down, we twain,
To the deeds of the field and the fold and the merry summer's gain.

Ah thus, only thus shall I see her, in dreams of the day or the night,
When my soul is beguiled of its sorrow to remember past delight.
She is gone. She was and she is not; there is no such thing on the earth
But e'en as a picture painted; and for me there is void and dearth
That I cannot name or measure.
                            Yet for me and all these she died,
E'en as she lived for awhile, that the better day might betide.
Therefore I live, and I shall live till the last day's work shall fail.
Have patience now but a little and I will tell you the tale
Of how and why she died, and why I am weak and worn,
And have wandered away to the meadows and the place where I was born:
But here and to-day I cannot; for ever my thought will stray
To that hope fulfilled for a little and the bliss of the earlier day.
Of the great world's hope and anguish to-day I scarce can think:
Like a ghost from the lives of the living and their earthly deeds I shrink.
I will go adown by the water and over the ancient bridge,
And wend in our footsteps of old till I come to the sun-burnt ridge,
And the great trench digged by the Romans; and thence awhile will I gaze,
And see three teeming counties stretch out till they fade in the haze;
And in all the dwellings of man that thence mine eyes shall see,
What man as hapless as I am beneath the sun shall be?

O fool, what words are these? Thou hast a sorrow to nurse,
And thou hast been bold and happy; but these, if they utter a curse,
No sting it has and no meaning—it is empty sound on the air.
Thy life is full of mourning, and theirs so empty and bare

That they have no words of complaining; nor so happy have they been
That they may measure sorrow or tell what grief may mean.
And thou, thou hast deeds to do, and toil to meet thee soon;
Depart and ponder on these through the sun-worn afternoon.

IX

A NEW FRIEND

I HAVE promised to tell you the story of how I was left alone
Sick and wounded and sore, and why the woman is gone
That I deemed a part of my life. Tell me when all is told,
If you deem it fit that the earth, that the world of men should hold
My work and my weariness still; yet think of that other life,
The child of me and of her, and the years and the coming strife.

After I came out of prison our living was hard to earn
By the work of my hands, and of hers; to shifts we had to turn,
Such as the poor know well, and the rich cannot understand,
And just out of the gutter we stood, still loving and hand in hand.

Do you ask me if still amidst all I held the hunt in view,
And the hope of the morning of life, all the things I should do and undo?
Be easy, I am not a coward: nay little prudence I learned,
I spoke and I suffered for speaking, and my meat by my manhood was burned.
When the poor man thinks—and rebels, the whip lies ready anear;
But he who is rebel and rich may live safe for many a year,
While he warms his heart with pictures of all the glory to come.
There's the storm of the press and the critics maybe, but sweet is his home,
There is meat in the morn and the even, and rest when the day is done,
All is fair and orderly there as the rising and setting sun—

And I know both the rich and the poor.

Well, I grew bitter they said;
'Tis not unlike that I did, for bitter indeed was my bread,
And surely the nursling plant shall smack of its nourishing soil.
And here was our life in short, pinching and worry and toil,
One petty fear thrust out by another come in its place,
Each scrap of life but a fear, and the sum of it wretched and base.
E'en so fare millions of men, where men for money are made,
Where the poor are dumb and deedless, where the rich are not afraid.
Ah, am I bitter again? Well, these are our breeding-stock,
The very base of order, and the state's foundation rock;
Is it so good and so safe that their manhood should be outworn
By the struggle for anxious life, the dull pain dismally borne,
Till all that was man within them is dead and vanished away?
Were it not even better that all these should think on a day
As they look on each other's sad faces, and see how many they are:
"What are these tales of old time of men who were mighty in war?
They fought for some city's dominion, for the name of a forest or field;
They fell that no alien's token should be blazoned on their shield;
And for this is their valour praised and dear is their renown,
And their names are beloved for ever and they wear the patriot's crown;
And shall we then wait in the streets and this heap of misery,
Till their stones rise up to help us or the far heavens set us free?
For we, we shall fight for no name, no blazon on banner or shield;
But that man to man may hearken and the earth her increase yield;
That never again in the world may be sights like we have seen;
That never again in the world may be men like we have been,
That never again like ours may be manhood spoilt and blurred."

Yea even so was I bitter, and this was my evilest word:
"Spend and be spent for our hope, and you at least shall be free,
Though you be rugged and coarse, as wasted and worn as you be."

Well, "bitter" I was, and denounced, and scarcely at last might we stand
From out of the very gutter, as we wended hand in hand.
I had written before for the papers, but so "bitter" was I grown,
That none of them now would have me that could pay me half-a-crown,
And the worst seemed closing around us; when as it needs must chance,
I spoke at some Radical Club of the Great Revolution in France.
Indeed I said nothing new to those who had learned it all,
And yet as something strange on some of the folk did it fall.
It was late in the terrible war, and France to the end drew nigh,
And some of us stood agape to see how the war would die,
And what would spring from its ashes. So when the talk was o'er
And after the stir and excitement I felt the burden I bore
Heavier yet for it all, there came to speak to me
A serious well-dressed man, a "gentleman," young I could see;
And we fell to talk together, and he shyly gave me praise,
And asked, though scarcely in words, of my past and my "better days."
Well, there,—I let it all out, and I flushed as I strode along,
(For we were walking by now) and bitterly spoke of the wrong.
Maybe I taught him something, but ready he was to learn,
And had come to our workmen meetings some knowledge of men to learn.
He kindled afresh at my words, although to try him I spake
More roughly than I was wont; but every word did he take
For what it was really worth, nor even laughter he spared,
As though he would look on life of its rags of habit bared.

Well, why should I be ashamed that he helped me at my need?
My wife and my child, must I kill them? And the man was a friend indeed,
And the work that he got me I did (it was writing, you understand)
As well as another might do it. To be short, he joined our band
Before many days were over, and we saw him everywhere
That we workmen met together, though I brought him not to my lair.
Eager he grew for the Cause, and we twain grew friend and friend:

He was dainty of mind and of body; most brave, as he showed in the end;
Merry despite of his sadness, quick-witted and speedy to see:
Like a perfect knight of old time as the poets would have them to be.
That was the friend that I won by my bitter speech at last.
He loved me; he grieved my soul: now the love and the grief are past;
He is gone with his eager learning, his sadness and his mirth,
His hope and his fond desire. There is no such thing on the earth.
He died not unbefriended—nor unbeloved maybe.
Betwixt my life and his longing there rolls a boundless sea.
And what are those memories now to all that I have to do,
The deeds to be done so many, the days of my life so few?

X

READY TO DEPART

I SAID of my friend new-found that at first he saw not my lair;
Yet he and I and my wife were together here and there;
And at last as my work increased and my den to a dwelling grew,
He came there often enough, and yet more together we drew.
Then came a change in the man; for a month he kept away,
Then came again and was with us for a fortnight every day,
But often he sat there silent, which was little his wont with us.
And at first I had no inkling of what constrained him thus;
I might have thought that he faltered, but now and again there came,
When we spoke of the Cause and its doings, a flash of his eager flame,
And he seemed himself for a while; then the brightness would fade away,
And he gloomed and shrank from my eyes.
                                    Thus passed day after day,
And grieved I grew, and I pondered: till at last one eve we sat
In the fire-lit room together, and talked of this and that,
But chiefly indeed of the war and what would come of it;
For Paris drew near to its fall, and wild hopes 'gan to flit
Amidst us Communist folk; and we talked of what might be done
When the Germans had gone their ways and the two were left alone,
Betrayers and betrayed in war-worn wasted France.

As I spoke the word "betrayed," my eyes met his in a glance,

And swiftly he turned away; then back with a steady gaze
He turned on me; and it seemed as when a sword-point plays
Round the sword in a battle's beginning and the coming on of strife.
For I knew though he looked on me, he saw not me, but my wife:
And he reddened up to the brow, and the tumult of the blood
Nigh blinded my eyes for a while, that I scarce saw bad or good,
Till I knew that he was arisen and had gone without a word.
Then I turned about unto her, and a quivering voice I heard
Like music without a meaning, and twice I heard my name.
"O Richard, Richard!" she said, and her arms about me came,
And her tears and the lips that I loved were on my face once more.
A while I clung to her body, and longing sweet and sore
Beguiled my heart of its sorrow; then we sundered and sore she wept,
While fair pictures of days departed about my sad heart crept,
And mazed I felt and weary. But we sat apart again,
Not speaking, while between us was the sharp and bitter pain
As the sword 'twixt the lovers bewildered in the fruitless marriage bed.
Yet a while, and we spoke together, and I scarce knew what I said,
But it was not wrath or reproaching, or the chill of love-born hate;
For belike around and about us, we felt the brooding fate.
We were gentle and kind together, and if any had seen us so,
They had said, "These two are one in the face of all trouble and woe."
But indeed as a wedded couple we shrank from the eyes of men,
As we dwelt together and pondered on the days that come not again.

Days passed and we dwelt together; nor Arthur came for awhile;
Gravely it was and sadly, and with no greeting smile,
That we twain met at our meetings: but no growth of hate was yet,
Though my heart at first would be sinking as our thoughts and our eyes
    they met:
And when he spake amidst us and as one we two agreed,
And I knew of his faith and his wisdom, then sore was my heart indeed.

We shrank from meeting alone: for the words we had to say
Our thoughts would nowise fashion—not yet for many a day.

Unhappy days of all days! Yet O might they come again!
So sore as my longing returneth to their trouble and sorrow and pain!

But time passed, and once we were sitting, my wife and I in our room,
And it was in the London twilight and the February gloom,
When there came a knock, and he entered all pale, though bright were
   his eyes,
And I knew that something had happened, and my heart to my mouth
   did arise.
"It is over," he said "—and beginning; for Paris has fallen at last,
And who knows what next shall happen after all that has happened and
   passed?
There now may we all be wanted."
                              I took up the word: "Well then
Let us go, we three together, and there to die like men."

"Nay," he said, "to live and be happy like men." Then he flushed up red,
And she no less as she hearkened, as one thought through their bodies
   had sped.
Then I reached out my hand unto him, and I kissed her once on the brow,
But no word craving forgiveness, and no word of pardon e'en now,
Our minds for our mouths might fashion.
                              In the February gloom
And into the dark we sat planning, and there was I in the room,
And in speech I gave and I took; but yet alone and apart
In the fields where I once was a youngling whiles wandered the thoughts
   of my heart,
And whiles in the unseen Paris, and the streets made ready for war.
Night grew and we lit the candles, and we drew together more,

And whiles we differed a little as we settled what to do,
And my soul was cleared of confusion as nigher the deed-time drew.

Well, I took my child into the country, as we had settled there,
And gave him o'er to be cherished by a kindly woman's care,
A friend of my mother's, but younger: and for Arthur, I let him give
His money, as mine was but little, that the boy might flourish and live,
Lest we three, or I and Arthur, should perish in tumult and war,
And at least the face of his father he should look on never more.
You cry out shame on my honour? But yet remember again
That a man in my boy was growing; must my passing pride and pain
Undo the manhood within him and his days and their doings blight?
So I thrust my pride away, and I did what I deemed was right,
And left him down in our country.
                              And well may you think indeed
How my sad heart swelled at departing from the peace of river and mead,
But I held all sternly aback and again to the town did I pass.
And as alone I journeyed, this was ever in my heart:
"They may die; they may live and be happy; but for me I know my part,
In Paris to do my utmost, and there in Paris to die!"
And I said, "The day of the deeds and the day of deliverance is nigh."

XI

A GLIMPSE OF THE COMING DAY

It was strange indeed, that journey! Never yet had I crossed the sea
Or looked on another people than the folk that had fostered me,
And my heart rose up and fluttered as in the misty night
We came on the fleet of the fishers slow rolling in the light
Of the hidden moon, as the sea dim under the false dawn lay;
And so like shadows of ships through the night they faded away,
And Calais pier was upon us. Dreamlike it was indeed
As we sat in the train together, and toward the end made speed.
But a dull sleep came upon me, and through the sleep a dream
Of the Frenchman who once was my master by the side of the willowy
    stream;
And he talked and told me tales of the war unwaged as yet,
And the victory never won, and bade me never forget,
While I walked on, still unhappy, by the home of the dark-striped perch.
Till at last, with a flash of light and a rattle and side-long lurch,
I woke up dazed and witless, till my sorrow awoke again,
And the grey of the morn was upon us as we sped through the poplar plain,
By the brimming streams and the houses with their grey roofs warped
    and bent,
And the horseless plough in the furrow, and things fair and innocent.
And there sat my wife before me, and she, too, dreamed as she slept;
For the slow tears fell from her eyelids as in her sleep she wept.

47

But Arthur sat by my side and waked; and flushed was his face,
And his eyes were quick to behold the picture of each fair place
That we flashed by as on we hurried; and I knew that the joy of life
Was strongly stirred within him by the thought of the coming strife.
Then I too thought for a little, It is good in grief's despite,
It is good to see earth's pictures, and so live in the day and the light.
Yea, we deemed that to death we were hastening, and it made our vision
    clear,
And we knew the delight of our life-days, and held their sorrow dear.

But now when we came unto Paris and were out in the sun and the street,
It was strange to see the faces that our wondering eyes did meet;
Such joy and peace and pleasure! That folk were glad we knew,
But knew not the why and the wherefore; and we who had just come
    through
The vanquished land and down-cast, and there at St. Denis e'en now
Had seen the German soldiers, and heard their bugles blow,
And the drum and fife go rattling through the freshness of the morn—
Yet here we beheld all joyous the folk they had made forlorn!
So at last from a grey stone building we saw a great flag fly,
One colour, red and solemn 'gainst the blue of the spring-tide sky,
And we stopped and turned to each other, and as each at each did we gaze,
The city's hope enwrapped us with joy and great amaze.

As folk in a dream we washed and we ate, and in all detail,
Oft told and in many a fashion, did we have all yesterday's tale:
How while we were threading our tangle of trouble in London there,
And I for my part, let me say it, within but a step of despair,
In Paris the day of days had betid; for the vile dwarf's stroke,
To madden Paris and crush her, had been struck and the dull sword broke;
There was now no foe and no fool in the city, and Paris was free;
And e'en as she is this morning, to-morrow all France will be.

We heard, and our hearts were saying, "In a little while all the earth—"
And that day at last of all days I knew what life was worth;
For I saw what few have beheld, a folk with all hearts gay.
Then at last I knew indeed that our word of the coming day,
That so oft in grief and in sorrow I had preached, and scarcely knew
If it was but despair of the present or the hope of the day that was due—
I say that I saw it now, real, solid and at hand.

And strange how my heart went back to our little nook of the land,
And how plain and clear I saw it, as though I longed indeed
To give it a share of the joy and the satisfaction of need
That here in the folk I beheld. For this in our country spring
Did the starlings bechatter the gables, and the thrush in the thorn-bush sing,
And the green cloud spread o'er the willows, and the little children rejoice
And shout midst a nameless longing to the morning's mingled voice;
For this was the promise of spring-tide, and the new leaves longing to burst,
And the white roads threading the acres, and the sun-warmed meadows
    athirst.
Once all was the work of sorrow and the life without reward,
And the toil that fear hath bidden, and the folly of master and lord;
But now are all things changing, and hope without a fear
Shall speed us on through the story of the changes of the year.
Now spring shall pluck the garland that summer weaves for all,
And autumn spread the banquet and winter fill the hall.
O earth, thou kind bestower, thou ancient fruitful place,
How lovely and beloved now gleams thy happy face!

And O mother, mother, I said, hadst thou known as I lay in thy lap,
And for me thou hopedst and fearedst, on what days my life should hap,
Hadst thou known of the death that I look for, and the deeds wherein I
    should deal,
How calm had been thy gladness! How sweet hadst thou smiled on my weal!

D

As some woman of old hadst thou wondered, who hath brought forth a
   god of the earth,
And in joy that knoweth no speech she dreams of the happy birth.

Yea, fair were those hours indeed, whatever hereafter might come,
And they swept over all my sorrow, and all thought of my wildered home.
But not for dreams of rejoicing had we come across the sea:
That day we delivered the letters that our friends had given to me,
And we craved for some work for the cause. And what work was there
   indeed,
But to learn the business of battle and the manner of dying at need?
We three could think of none other, and we wrought our best therein;
And both of us made a shift the sergeant's stripes to win,
For diligent were we indeed: and he, as in all he did,
Showed a cheerful ready talent that nowise might be hid,
And yet hurt the pride of no man that he needs must step before.
But as for my wife, the *brancard* of the ambulance-women she wore,
And gently and bravely would serve us; and to all as a sister to be—
A sister amidst of the strangers—and, alas! a sister to me.

XII

MEETING THE WAR-MACHINE

So we dwelt in the war-girdled city as a very part of its life.
Looking back at it all from England, I an atom of the strife,
I can see that I might have seen what the end would be from the first,
The hope of man devoured in the day when the Gods are athirst.
But those days we lived, as I tell you, a life that was not our own;
And we saw but the hope of the world, and the seed that the ages had sown,
Spring up now a fair-blossomed tree from the earth lying over the dead;
Earth quickened, earth kindled to spring-tide with the blood that her
   lovers have shed,
With the happy days cast off for the sake of her happy day,
With the love of women foregone, and the bright youth worn away,
With the gentleness stripped from the lives thrust into the jostle of war,
With the hope of the hardy heart forever dwindling afar.

O Earth, Earth, look on thy lovers, who knew all thy gifts and thy gain,
But cast them aside for thy sake, and caught up barren pain!
Indeed of some art thou mindful, and ne'er shalt forget their tale,
Till shrunk are the floods of thine ocean and thy sun is waxen pale.
But rather I bid thee remember e'en these of the latter days,
Who were fed by no fair promise and made drunken by no praise.
For them no opening heaven reached out the martyr's crown;
No folk delivered wept them, and no harvest of renown

They reaped with the scythe of battle; nor round their dying bed
Did kindly friendly farewell the dew of blessing shed;
In the sordid streets of the city mid a folk that knew them not,
In the living death of the prison didst thou deal them out their lot,
Yet foundest them deeds to be doing; and no feeble folk were they
To scowl on their own undoing and wail their lives away;
But oft were they blithe and merry and deft from the strife to wring
Some joy that others gained not midst their peaceful wayfaring.
So fared they, giftless ever, and no help of fortune sought.
Their life was thy deliverance, O Earth, and for thee they fought;
Mid the jeers of the happy and deedless, mid failing friends they went
To their foredoomed fruitful ending on the love of thee intent.

Yea and we were a part of it all, the beginning of the end,
That first fight of the uttermost battle whither all the nations wend;
And yet could I tell you its story, you might think it little and mean.
For few of you now will be thinking of the day that might have been,
And fewer still meseemeth of the day that yet shall be,
That shall light up that first beginning and its tangled misery.
For indeed a very machine is the war that now men wage;
Nor have we hold of its handle, we gulled of our heritage,
We workmen slaves of machines. Well, it ground us small enough
This machine of the beaten Bourgeois; though oft the work was rough
That it turned out for its money. Like other young soldiers at first
I scarcely knew the wherefore why our side had had the worst;
For man to man and in knots we faced the matter well;
And I thought, well to-morrow or next day a new tale will be to tell.
I was fierce and not afraid; yet O were the wood-sides fair,
And the crofts and the sunny gardens, though death they harboured there!
And few but fools are fain of leaving the world outright,
And the story over and done, and an end of the life and the light.
No hatred of life, thou knowest, O Earth, mid the bullets I bore,

Though pain and grief oppressed me that I never may suffer more.
But in those days past over did life and death seem one;
Yea the life had we attained to which could never be undone.

You would have me tell of the fighting? Well, you know it was new to me,
Yet it soon seemed as if it had been for ever, and ever would be.
The morn when we made that sally, some thought (and yet not I)
That a few days and all would be over: just a few had got to die,
And the rest would be happy thenceforward. But my stubborn country blood
Was bidding me hold my halloo till we were out of the wood.
And that was the reason perhaps why little disheartened I was,
As we stood all huddled together that night in a helpless mass,
As beaten men are wont: and I knew enough of war
To know midst its unskilled labour what slips full often are.

There was Arthur unhurt beside me, and my wife come back again,
And surely that eve between us there was love though no lack of pain
As we talked all the matter over, and our hearts spake more than our lips;
And we said, "We shall learn, we shall learn—yea, e'en from disasters
    and slips."

Well, many a thing we learned, but we learned not how to prevail
O'er the brutal war-machine, the ruthless grinder of bale;
By the bourgeois world it was made, for the bourgeois world; and we,
We were e'en as the village weaver 'gainst the power-loom, maybe.
It drew on nearer and nearer, and we 'gan to look to the end—
We three, at least—and our lives began with death to blend;
Though we were long a-dying—though I dwell on yet as a ghost
In the land where we once were happy, to look on the loved and the lost.

XIII

THE STORY'S ENDING

How can I tell you the story of the Hope and its defence?
We wrought in a narrow circle; it was hither and thither and thence;
To the walls, and back for a little; to the fort and there to abide,
Grey-beards and boys and women; they lived there—and they died;
Nor counted much in the story. I have heard it told since then,
And mere lies our deeds have turned to in the mouths of happy men,
And e'en those will be soon forgotten as the world wends on its way,
Too busy for truth or kindness. Yet my soul is seeing the day
When those who are now but children the new generation shall be,
And e'en in our land of commerce and the workshop over the sea,
Amid them shall spring up the story; yea the very breath of the air
To the yearning hearts of the workers true tale of it all shall bear.
Year after year shall men meet with the red flag over head,
And shall call on the help of the vanquished and the kindness of the dead.
And time that weareth most things, and the years that overgrow
The tale of the fools triumphant, yet clearer and clearer shall show
The deeds of the helpers of menfolk to every age and clime,
The deeds of the cursed and the conquered that were wise before their
  time.

Of these were my wife and my friend; there they ended their wayfaring
Like the generations before them thick thronging as leaves of the spring,
Fast falling as leaves of the autumn as the ancient singer hath said,
And each one with a love and a story. Ah the grief of the early dead!

"What is all this talk?" you are saying; "why all this long delay?"
Yes, indeed, it is hard in the telling. Of things too grievous to say
I would be, but cannot be, silent. Well, I hurry on to the end—
For it drew to the latter ending of the hope that we helped to defend.
The forts were gone and the foemen drew near to the thin-manned wall,
And it wanted not many hours to the last hour and the fall,
And we lived amid the bullets and seldom went away
To what as yet were the streets by night-tide or by day.
We three, we fought together, and I did the best I could,
Too busy to think of the ending; but Arthur was better than good;
Resourceful, keen and eager, from post to post he ran,
To thrust out aught that was moving and bring up the uttermost man,
He was gone on some such errand, and was absent a little space,
When I turned about for a moment and saw my wife's fair face,
And her foot set firm on the rampart, as she hastened here and there,
To some of our wounded comrades such help as she could to bear.
Then straight she looked upon me with such lovely, friendly eyes
Of the days gone by and remembered, that up from my heart 'gan rise
The choking sobbing passion; but I kept it aback, and smiled,
And waved my hand aloft—But therewith her face turned wild
In a moment of time, and she stared along the length of the wall,
And I saw a man who was running and crouching, stagger and fall,
And knew it for Arthur at once; but voiceless toward him she ran,
I with her, crying aloud. But or ever we reached the man,
Lo! a roar and a crash around us and my sick brain whirling around,
And a white light turning to black, and no sky and no air and no ground,
And then what I needs must tell of as a great blank; but indeed
No words to tell of its horror hath language for my need:
As a map is to a picture, so is all that my words can say.

But when I came to myself, in a friend's house sick I lay
Amid strange blended noises, and my own mind wandering there;

Delirium in me indeed and around me everywhere.
That passed, and all things grew calmer, I with them: all the stress
That the last three months had been on me now sank to helplessness.
I bettered, and then they told me the tale of what had betid;
And first, that under the name of a friend of theirs I was hid,
Who was slain by mere misadventure, and was English as was I,
And no rebel, and had due papers wherewith I might well slip by
When I was somewhat better. Then I knew, though they had not told,
How all was fallen together, and my heart grew sick and cold.
And yet indeed thenceforward I strove my life to live,
That e'en as I was and so hapless I yet might live to strive.
It was but few words they told me of that murder great and grim,
And how with the blood of the guiltless the city's streets did swim,
And of other horrors they told not, except in a word or two,
When they told of their scheme to save me from the hands of the
    villainous crew,
Whereby I guessed what was happening in the main without detail.
And so at last it came to their telling the other tale
Of my wife and my friend; though that also methought I knew too well.
Well, they said that I had been wounded by the fragment of a shell,
Another of which had slain her outright, as forth she ran
Toward Arthur struck by a bullet. She never touched the man
Alive and she also alive; but thereafter as they lay
Both dead on one litter together, then folk who knew not us,
But were moved by seeing the twain so fair and so piteous,
Took them for husband and wife who were fated there to die,
Or, it may be lover and lover indeed—but what know I?

Well, you know that I 'scaped from Paris, and crossed the narrow sea,
And made my way to the country where we twain were wont to be,
And that is the last and the latest of the tale I have to tell.
I came not here to be bidding my happiness farewell,

And to nurse my grief and to win me the gain of a wounded life,
That because of the bygone sorrow may hide away from the strife.
I came to look to my son, and myself to get stout and strong,
That two men there might be hereafter to battle against the wrong;
And I cling to the love of the past and the love of the day to be,
And the present, it is but the building of the man to be strong in me.

CHANTS FOR SOCIALISTS

THE DAY IS COMING

Come hither, lads, and hearken, for a tale there is to tell,
Of the wonderful days a-coming, when all shall be better than well.

And the tale shall be told of a country, a land in the midst of the sea,
And folk shall call it England in the days that are going to be.

There more than one in a thousand in the days that are yet to come
Shall have some hope of the morrow, some joy of the ancient home.

For then—laugh not, but listen to this strange tale of mine—
All folk that are in England shall be better lodged than swine.

Then a man shall work and bethink him, and rejoice in the deeds of his
    hand,
Nor yet come home in the even too faint and weary to stand.

Men in that time a-coming shall work and have no fear
For to-morrow's lack of earning and the hunger-wolf anear.

I tell you this for a wonder, that no man then shall be glad
Of his fellow's fall and mishap to snatch at the work he had.

For that which the worker winneth shall then be his indeed,
Nor shall half be reaped for nothing by him that sowed no seed.

O strange new wonderful justice! But for whom shall we gather the gain?
For ourselves and for each of our fellows, and no hand shall labour in vain.

Then all Mine and all Thine shall be Ours, and no more shall any man crave
For riches that serve for nothing but to fetter a friend for a slave.

And what wealth then shall be left us when none shall gather gold
To buy his friend in the market, and pinch and pine the sold?

Nay, what save the lovely city, and the little house on the hill,
And the wastes and the woodland beauty, and the happy fields we till;

And the homes of ancient stories, the tombs of the mighty dead;
And the wise men seeking out marvels, and the poet's teeming head;

And the painter's hand of wonder; and the marvellous fiddle-bow,
And the banded choirs of music: all those that do and know.

For all these shall be ours and all men's, nor shall any lack a share
Of the toil and the gain of living in the days when the world grows fair.

Ah! such are the days that shall be! But what are the deeds of to-day,
In the days of the years we dwell in, that wear our lives away?

Why, then, and for what are we waiting? There are three words to speak:
WE WILL IT, and what is the foeman but the dream-strong wakened and
    weak?

O why and for what are we waiting? while our brothers droop and die,
And on every wind of the heavens a wasted life goes by.

How long shall they reproach us where crowd on crowd they dwell,
Poor ghosts of the wicked city, the gold-crushed hungry hell?

Through squalid life they laboured, in sordid grief they died,
Those sons of a mighty mother, those props of England's pride.

They are gone; there is none can undo it, nor save our souls from the curse;
But many a million cometh, and shall they be better or worse?

It is we must answer and hasten, and open wide the door
For the rich man's hurrying terror, and the slow-foot hope of the poor.

Yea, the voiceless wrath of the wretched, and their unlearned discontent,
We must give it voice and wisdom till the waiting-tide be spent.

Come, then, since all things call us, the living and the dead,
And o'er the weltering tangle a glimmering light is shed.

Come, then, let us cast off fooling, and put by ease and rest,
For the CAUSE alone is worthy till the good days bring the best.

Come, join in the only battle wherein no man can fail,
Where whoso fadeth and dieth, yet his deed shall still prevail.

Ah! come, cast off all fooling, for this, at least, we know:
That the Dawn and the Day is coming, and forth the Banners go.

THE VOICE OF TOIL

I HEARD men saying, Leave hope and praying,
　　All days shall be as all have been;
To-day and to-morrow bring fear and sorrow,
　　The never-ending toil between.

When Earth was younger mid toil and hunger,
　　In hope we strove, and our hands were strong;
Then great men led us, with words they fed us,
　　And bade us right the earthly wrong.

Go read in story their deeds and glory,
　　Their names amidst the nameless dead;
Turn then from lying to us slow-dying
　　In that good world to which they led;

Where fast and faster our iron master,
　　The thing we made, for ever drives,
Bids us grind treasure and fashion pleasure
　　For other hopes and other lives.

E

Where home is a hovel and dull we grovel,
  Forgetting that the world is fair;
Where no babe we cherish, lest its very soul perish;
  Where our mirth is crime, our love a snare.

Who now shall lead us, what god shall heed us
  As we lie in the hell our hands have won?
For us are no rulers but fools and befoolers,
  The great are fallen, the wise men gone.

I heard men saying, Leave tears and praying,
  The sharp knife heedeth not the sheep;
Are we not stronger than the rich and the wronger,
  When day breaks over dreams and sleep?

Come, shoulder to shoulder ere the world grows older!
  Help lies in nought but thee and me;
Hope is before us, the long years that bore us
  Bore leaders more than men may be.

Let dead hearts tarry and trade and marry,
  And trembling nurse their dreams of mirth,
While we the living our lives are giving
  To bring the bright new world to birth.

Come, shoulder to shoulder ere earth grows older
  The Cause spreads over land and sea;
Now the world shaketh, and fear awaketh
  And joy at last for thee and me.

NO MASTER

SAITH man to man, We've heard and known
   That we no master need
To live upon this earth, our own,
   In fair and manly deed.
The grief of slaves long passed away
   For us hath forged the chain,
Till now each worker's patient day
   Builds up the House of Pain.

And we, shall we too, crouch and quail,
   Ashamed, afraid of strife,
And lest our lives untimely fail
   Embrace the Death in Life?
Nay, cry aloud, and have no fear,
   We few against the world;
Awake, arise! the hope we bear
   Against the curse is hurled.

It grows and grows—are we the same,
   The feeble band, the few?
Or what are these with eyes aflame,
   And hands to deal and do?
This is the host that bears the word,
   NO MASTER HIGH OR LOW—
A lightning flame, a shearing sword,
   A storm to overthrow.

ALL FOR THE CAUSE

HEAR a word, a word in season, for the day is drawing nigh,
When the Cause shall call upon us, some to live, and some to die!

He that dies shall not die lonely, many an one hath gone before;
He that lives shall bear no burden heavier than the life they bore.

Nothing ancient is their story, e'en but yesterday they bled,
Youngest they of earth's beloved, last of all the valiant dead.

E'en the tidings we are telling was the tale they had to tell,
E'en the hope that our hearts cherish, was the hope for which they fell.

In the grave where tyrants thrust them, lies their labour and their pain,
But undying from their sorrow springeth up the hope again.

Mourn not therefore, nor lament it, that the world outlives their life;
Voice and vision yet they give us, making strong our hands for strife.

Some had name, and fame, and honour, learn'd they were, and wise and
    strong;
Some were nameless, poor, unlettered, weak in all but grief and wrong.

Named and nameless all live in us; one and all they lead us yet
Every pain to count for nothing, every sorrow to forget.

Hearken how they cry, "O happy, happy ye that ye were born
In the sad slow night's departing, in the rising of the morn.

"Fair the crown the Cause hath for you, well to die or well to live
Through the battle, through the tangle, peace to gain or peace to give."

Ah, it may be! Oft meseemeth, in the days that yet shall be,
When no slave of gold abideth 'twixt the breadth of sea to sea,

Oft, when men and maids are merry, ere the sunlight leaves the earth,
And they bless the day beloved, all too short for all their mirth,

Some shall pause awhile and ponder on the bitter days of old,
Ere the toil of strife and battle overthrew the curse of gold;

Then 'twixt lips of loved and lover solemn thoughts of us shall rise;
We who once were fools and dreamers, then shall be the brave and wise.

There amidst the world new-builded shall our earthly deeds abide,
Though our names be all forgotten, and the tale of how we died.

Life or death then, who shall heed it, what we gain or what we lose?
Fair flies life amid the struggle, and the Cause for each shall choose.

Hear a word, a word in season, for the day is drawing nigh,
When the Cause shall call upon us, some to live, and some to die!

THE MARCH OF THE WORKERS

WHAT is this, the sound and rumour? What is this that all men hear,
Like the wind in hollow valleys when the storm is drawing near,
Like the rolling on of ocean in the eventide of fear?
                              'Tis the people marching on.

Whither go they, and whence come they? What are these of whom ye
    tell?
In what country are they dwelling 'twixt the gates of heaven and hell?
Are they mine or thine for money? Will they serve a master well?
                              Still the rumour's marching on.

        Hark the rolling of the thunder!
        Lo the sun! and lo thereunder
        Riseth wrath, and hope, and wonder,
                              And the host comes marching on.

Forth they come from grief and torment; on they wend toward health
    and mirth,
All the wide world is their dwelling, every corner of the earth.
Buy them, sell them for thy service! Try the bargain what 'tis worth,
                              For the days are marching on.

These are they who build thy houses, weave thy raiment, win thy wheat,
Smooth the rugged, fill the barren, turn the bitter into sweet,
All for thee this day—and ever. What reward for them is meet
                    Till the host comes marching on?

        Hark the rolling of the thunder!
        Lo the sun! and lo thereunder
        Riseth wrath, and hope, and wonder,
                And the host comes marching on.

Many a hundred years passed over have they laboured deaf and blind;
Never tidings reached their sorrow, never hope their toil might find.
Now at last they've heard and hear it, and the cry comes down the wind,
                And their feet are marching on.

O ye rich men hear and tremble! for with words the sound is rife:
"Once for you and death we laboured; changed henceforward is the
    strife.
We are men, and we shall battle for the world of men and life;
                And our host is marching on."

        Hark the rolling of the thunder!
        Lo the sun! and lo thereunder
        Riseth wrath, and hope, and wonder,
                And the host comes marching on.

"Is it war, then? Will ye perish as the dry wood in the fire?
Is it peace? Then be ye of us, let your hope be our desire.
Come and live! for life awaketh, and the world shall never tire;
                And hope is marching on.

"On we march then, we the workers, and the rumour that ye hear
Is the blended sound of battle and deliv'rance drawing near;
For the hope of every creature is the banner that we bear,
                    And the world is marching on."

          Hark the rolling of the thunder!
          Lo the sun! and lo thereunder
          Riseth wrath, and hope, and wonder,
                    And the host comes marching on.

DOWN AMONG THE DEAD MEN

COME, comrades, come, your glasses clink;
Up with your hands a health to drink,
The health of all that workers be,
In every land, on every sea.
    And he that will this health deny,
    Down among the dead men, down among the dead men,
    Down, down, down, down,
    Down among the dead men let him lie!

Well done! now drink another toast,
And pledge the gath'ring of the host,
The people armed in brain and hand,
To claim their rights in every land.
    And he that will, etc.

There's liquor left; come, let's be kind,
And drink the rich a better mind,
That when we knock upon the door,
They may be off and say no more.
    And he that will, etc.

E 2

Now, comrades, let the glass blush red,
Drink we the unforgotten dead
That did their deeds and went away,
Before the bright sun brought the day.
　　And he that will, etc.

The Day? Ah, friends, late grows the night;
Drink to the glimmering spark of light,
The herald of the joy to be,
The battle-torch of thee and me!
　　And he that will, etc.

Take yet another cup in hand
And drink in hope our little band;
Drink strife in hope while lasteth breath,
And brotherhood in life and death;
　　And he that will this health deny,
　　Down among the dead men, down among the dead men,
　　Down, down, down, down,
　　Down among the dead men let him lie!

A DEATH SONG

WHAT cometh here from west to east awending?
And who are these, the marchers stern and slow?
We bear the message that the rich are sending
Aback to those who bade them wake and know.
Not one, not one, nor thousands must they slay,
But one and all if they would dusk the day.

We asked them for a life of toilsome earning,
They bade us bide their leisure for our bread;
We craved to speak to tell our woeful learning:
We come back speechless, bearing back our dead.
Not one, not one, nor thousands must they slay,
But one and all if they would dusk the day.

They will not learn; they have no ears to hearken.
They turn their faces from the eyes of fate;
Their gay-lit halls shut out the skies that darken.
But, lo! this dead man knocking at the gate.
Not one, not one, nor thousands must they slay,
But one and all if they would dusk the day.

A DEATH SONG

Here lies the sign that we shall break our prison;
Amidst the storm he won a prisoner's rest;
But in the cloudy dawn the sun arisen
Brings us our day of work to win the best.
Not one, not one, nor thousands must they slay,
But one and all if they would dusk the day.

MAY DAY [1892]

THE WORKERS.

O EARTH, once again cometh Spring to deliver
    Thy winter-worn heart, O thou friend of the Sun;
Fair blossom the meadows from river to river
    And the birds sing their triumph o'er winter undone.

O Earth, how a-toiling thou singest thy labour
    And upholdest the flower-crowned cup of thy bliss,
As when in the feast-tide drinks neighbour to neighbour
    And all words are gleeful, and nought is amiss.

But we, we, O Mother, through long generations,
    We have toiled and been fruitful, but never with thee
Might we raise up our bowed heads and cry to the nations
    To look on our beauty, and hearken our glee.

Unlovely of aspect, heart-sick and a-weary
    On the season's fair pageant all dim-eyed we gaze;
Of thy fairness we fashion a prison-house dreary
    And in sorrow wear over each day of our days.

THE EARTH.

O children! O toilers, what foemen beleaguer
  The House I have built you, the Home I have won?
Full great are my gifts, and my hands are all eager
  To fill every heart with the deeds I have done.

THE WORKERS.

The foemen are born of thy body, O Mother,
  In our shape are they shapen, their voice is the same;
And the thought of their hearts is as ours and no other;
  It is they of our own house that bring us to shame.

THE EARTH.

Are ye few? Are they many? What words have ye spoken
  To bid your own brethren remember the Earth?
What deeds have ye done that the bonds should be broken,
  And men dwell together in good-will and mirth?

THE WORKERS.

They are few, we are many: and yet, O our Mother,
  Many years were we wordless and nought was our deed,
But now the word flitteth from brother to brother:
  We have furrowed the acres and scattered the seed.

THE EARTH.

Win on then unyielding, through fair and foul weather,
  And pass not a day that your deed shall avail.

And in hope every spring-tide come gather together
  That unto the Earth ye may tell all your tale.

Then this shall I promise, that I am abiding
  The day of your triumph, the ending of gloom,
And no wealth that ye will then my hand shall be hiding
  And the tears of the spring into roses shall bloom.

MAY DAY, 1894

CLAD is the year in all her best,
    The land is sweet and sheen;
Now Spring with Summer at her breast,
    Goes down the meadows green.

Here are we met to welcome in
    The young abounding year,
To praise what she would have us win
    Ere winter draweth near.

For surely all is not in vain,
    This gallant show she brings;
But seal of hope and sign of gain,
    Beareth this Spring of springs.

No longer now the seasons wear
    Dull, without any tale
Of how the chain the toilers bear
    Is growing thin and frail.

But hope of plenty and goodwill
    Flies forth from land to land,
Nor any now the voice can still
    That crieth on the hand.

A little while shall Spring come back
   And find the Ancient Home
Yet marred by foolish waste and lack,
   And most enthralled by some.

A little while, and then at last
   Shall the greetings of the year
Be blent with wonder of the past
   And all the griefs that were.

A little while, and they that meet
   The living year to praise,
Shall be to them as music sweet
   That grief of bye-gone days.

So be we merry to our best,
   Now the land is sweet and sheen,
And Spring with Summer at her breast
   Goes down the meadows green.

PRINTED IN GREAT BRITAIN
BY BALLANTYNE, HANSON & CO. LTD.
EDINBURGH AND LONDON

CPSIA information can be obtained at www.ICGtesting.com
Printed in the USA
LVOW131646220412

278650LV00011B/11/P